FROM A DIARY

By Michael Hamburger from Anvil

POETRY

Roots in the Air
Collected Poems 1941–1994
Late
Intersections

TRANSLATIONS

PAUL CELAN: Poems
GOETHE: Poems and Epigrams
HÖLDERLIN: Poems and Fragments
RILKE: An Unofficial Rilke

CRITICISM

The Truth of Poetry

Michael Hamburger

From a Diary of Non-Events

ANVIL PRESS POETRY

Published in 2002
by Anvil Press Poetry Ltd
Neptune House 70 Royal Hill London SE10 8RF
www.anvilpresspoetry.com

Copyright © Michael Hamburger 2002

This book is published with financial assistance
from The Arts Council of England

Designed and set in Monotype Ehrhardt by Anvil
Printed and bound in England
by Cromwell Press, Trowbridge, Wiltshire

ISBN 0 85646 343 4

A catalogue record for this book
is available from the British Library

The author's moral rights have been asserted in accordance
with the Copyright, Designs and Patents Act 1988

All rights reserved

ACKNOWLEDGEMENTS

Parts of this poem have appeared in *Oasis*, *PN Review*, *Stand*
and the yearbook *Das Gedicht* (Germany).

CONTENTS

FROM A DIARY OF NON-EVENTS

December	9
January	11
February	13
March	16
April	20
May	24
June	28
July	31
August	38
September	43
October	50
November	56

From a Diary of Non-Events

DECEMBER

I

Sunshine on hoarfrost: one true winter day
After a whole year's cloudbursts, hurricane, drizzle,
Puddles on flowerbeds, the well-drained marsh a bog.

It's advertisers' Advent. GLOBAL WARNING
Where flood water creeps or sweeps, tall trees crashed down.

Outside this window residual birds are fed
Imported peanuts, packaged grain, assorted.
Rats have gnawed through
Another hardwood frame
To raid the apple store
As if no glut of fallen apples lay
On the rats' playground larger than room or house.
Or was it a squirrel so deregulated?
Those frames had lasted since the walls were built.

All's mending now, not making.
As beggared birds to gardens
Wildness draws in.
Their moors, their woods, their shores
Are less than the remembered.
From the near pasture plovers have vanished,
Snipe, red-legged partridge, skylark, thrush
Whose kinds were doubled in the wane of light,
Enriching it, left iciest winter true.

2

Lured by a virtual music,
Birdcalls clogged ears retain,
Abstract of what the seasons hid and held,
In mind alone I walk away from chores
Towards the sea, old matrix of all making
Depleted here of whales' meal, primal plankton,
Kelp jungle, mollusc, fish,
Capacious, though, as death, potential still.

Moonlight grows real again in these long nights,
Lets even land be real
For eyes that unreality estranged,
Promiscuous distraction dulled and dimmed.

I hear the barn-owl's wings, the never heard,
By them in starless darkness find my way.

JANUARY

Damped light. The daily lane.
Four times above it
The dubious bird,
And no binoculars on me.
A blackbird silhouette
But the tones leafless, bare
As where it perches, the high willow bough,
Not the accented phrase
That's small-talk still.
No stress, arpeggio, trill,
More monologue than call –
To whom, to whom whom whom, whom whom . . . –
And that continuous.
With quarter-tones in it?
If so, not for these damned iambics,
Not for noise-cluttered ears
Another 'elegy' for Edward Thomas's England,
His bird, the missel-thrush
Suburbanized even then, but commonly met,
Vernacular of the footpath, pavement, road.

Revenant now at best
In half-light, half-remembrance, half-recognition
Here, where by order once again
The skeletal hedgerows have been slashed
So that container trucks grown cottage-sized,
Tanker, delivery van
Suffer no damage, no delay

To their prefabricated bulk
Ever more smoothly coming, going, gone.

And in between, on the same willow bough,
This hint of a return the rumbling drowns.

FEBRUARY

I

Puddled, some snowdrops dangle,
The earlier aconites
Keep closed their petals that, sodden, soon will rot.
Only the hellebores, the purple, white,
Yes, and the stinking with leaf-coloured flowers
Like money-ridden politicians make to thrive
By the pretence of growth,
No longer what they seem, let alone nature,
Still with the name of Christmas rose defy
The new non-seasons, droopingly persistent.

For a few minutes the morning sun
Behind black columns blinks,
Shily, as though about to rise to it,
Put in a brief appearance . . .
Then the day drizzles on.

2

Catching me at my gloomy labours –
Who, helleborish too, defy
Messages of the soil, sea, sky –
'Look on the bright side!', say the neighbours.
I look, both to the left and right,
Forward and back: the only sight
That's brighter is a conflagration.
Ought I to tell them the location?
Consideration keeps me mum.
I hum and haw, I haw and hum,
Try hard to smile and don't confess
That a true owl's hoot chills me less
Than chirped complaisant cheerfulness.

3

This linden, fifteen years old, the root rain-loosened,
Inclines, a sallow sprawls.

Look long and low, the mutable winds advise:
What holds is microcosms, what is failing
Minds that could mirror them, but manipulate.
Rise early, and you'll see
Another fire, the red-hot sun all harmless
Lie on a field's horizon.
Though in occluded light, sap swells the buds,
Out of dark chrysalids new wings will creep,
Glistening, in any weather,
A whiteness into night, hazed rays passed on
Through clouds by the cold moon.

MARCH

I

Rain, snow, sleet in Alaskan winds and rain again
Broach the calendar month.
Intermissions of sunshine
Dupe one daffodil into flower
From a bulb become aquatic,
One plum-tree's bare boughs to open
Limp flowerlets to the abeyance of bees.
On both islands, in mainland Europe
Subrural remains have hit the headlines:
A plague on both Houses and any house,
Another setback to exports of food, imports of tourists,
Awkward reminder that goods are not raised or grown
In supermarkets, however processed for profit,
However transported, packaged,
Money's luxuriance, even now
Springs from *pecunia*, flocks and herds,
Their health and the health of their keepers.

And I, mere cultivator
Of unsaleable fruit,
Must fear for my non-events:
At any moment they could be news,
Like the slaughter, no longer scheduled, discreet
Of cattle, pigs and sheep,
Like the maize or rape plant mutated,
Like the non-climate, non-seasons too
When hurricane, earthquake, eruption, flood or drought
Has proved efficient as warfare,
As the managed destruction of habitats, populations.

2

White, white, white in the grey light,
Seen from a first-floor window, this pastureland
On which yesterday morning still familiar cows lay
    sleeping
Globally curves as the crust of Earth
Towards not the North Sea shore
But space itself, a horizon
Beyond the bounds of our tending.

To the south, on the white lawn
Three pheasants walk,
Survivors of the shoot,
Carriers no doubt of the virus life-and-death,
Searchers now for their fodder snowed over.

Soon a fox, the survivor
Of hunts and gamekeeper's gun,
Will be stalking them
Over the convex surface all white, white, white
Which, warmed, will uncover
Celandine, violet buds,
Feathers and bones shed.

3

Mild air flows in before one morning shines,
Lures toads to water
Across the tarmacked lane
Strewn overnight with the flattened corpses of those
An alien speed ripped from their season's need.

Even to blocked ears comes
The rat-tat-tat, spring-frenzied,
From a woodpecker's timber drum,
Louder and faster than
The hammering that resounded
An age ago from the village forge.

Cloud clots again, day-long, night-long drips
So that, if haste misled them,
The toads that crossed not in a water-ditch
But pool or puddle could be spawning,
Breeding for slow abortion in mere overflow.

4

Grey, grey the land's end, not yet with smoke from
    pyres,
Meets the sea's grey that merges
In a low cloud horizon, grey.
There vision, smudged, is lost
At the spring equinox of a dithering year
All mired and bogged while baffled senses wait
For the now cancerous rays
Which, hidden or too stark, still draw toads to water,
Sap out of sodden roots, wings into air,
From us, where seen and felt, the ambivalent
    answering fire.

Here, cows not yet culled huddle against
The mutilated skeleton of a whitethorn hedge
By order stripped of its bud-bearing boughs.
Through it a sleet-wind lashes.

APRIL

I

Fools' Day has tricked the diagnostic view:
A visible sun has risen
At the pasture's far end from a scud
Not smoke but vapour released at last
From ground long sodden, puddled.
Out of that wispy whiteness contours emerge,
The whiter white and black
Of the Frisian cows grazing as ever,
Prodigious now as a Gipsy encampment surprised
In a German glade in April 1945,
A congregation of Jews untagged
In the centre of ruined Dresden.
Here too eugenics, the money-driven,
Doomed the defenceless breeds
To be slaughtered for purity by butchers mortal, impure.

In the foreground, survivors at one remove,
A family outing of pheasants runs
From no threat of gun or fox
Where once it was peewits that fed and nested,
A black and white, a greener lustre responded in feathers lit.

2

Then three fine days, a regional idyll
Snatched from national need,
Public footpaths forbidden, beaches even closed,
The metaphysical signposts covered,
No alibi left to the urban seekers.

Overnight only, an intermission of rain,
So that like patches of ice new puddles shine
While a breeze non-malignantly blows from the south.

3

Towards Easter the morning mist
Is pregnant with a prayer
Become unspeakable, though, in words that are human:
That from the dominion of global greed
Absolute at the millennium's turn
When older and upstart empires
Had been subdued, dismembered
Or, bit by bit, taken over,
Delivered, a world will remain
Not quite as it was in the beginning;
That the moon will not be a screen
For advertisements flashed at her
By electronics, residual Earth
Not a commercial-financial-military site
Cleared of all creatures other
Than homo pseudo-sapiens,
Food factories more efficient
And such wildlife reservations
As that species may still require
For selected continuance
Once the billions have been reduced;
That the star war system be hoist
With its own petard, imploding
But leaving a matrix of life,
Nucleus of it, at least, unsplit.
For if as a daily occurrence
Doomsday has been doled out
Piecemeal, protracted, laborious,
So may the refounding be.

But if in their languages animals pray,
These plants, the stones and the mud, in silence,
Then hear their prayer, not the translation.

4

For a gabble of widowed words, all demented,
Fills the asylum Amnesia
That trades as 'Old Vocables' Home',
Their irrelevant records
Computerized in an office kept locked.

Open to anyone who can pay –
Except intractable cases:
Anthropomorphic misanthropists,
Those with perverse expectations,
Repressed public concerns
Or related hang-ups, anachronisms.

The staff go about their business
As though the naming sufficed
Where, uttered, a name's a logo
Disowned by Logos, the meaning.

Our special attraction:
Cacophonous chorus, daily.
Moribund solos, concurrent.
Haunting echoes of kinds extinct.

MAY

I

Against adverse winds the first swallows, house martins
Have strained their wings in migration.
A few have alighted, in adverse winds,
But cannot settle yet,
Cannot mend their diminished nests.

If somewhere one cuckoo calls
It's far off, a rumour disputed.
When the scurrying rainclouds break
It's a single butterfly still,
Sporadic sortie of orange-tip, peacock –

Tokens only of cyclic return.

Ape, elephant, dog
May mourn their kin – kin by transference also –
Cry out at unnatural wrong,
Cow for the calf taken from her.
But exempt from the selfhood that suffers time, its
    invention,
Animals know how to die –
One by one, by species, by genus
Which to maintain, transmute was their primal urge,
So to us making over
The burden of loss, become ours.

2

With no voice but the weather's,
Plants, the gross and delicate,
Indigenous, exotic, tree-sized, minute,
Have defied the non-season by thriving.
Set back, they prolong their flowering,
Primroses, here, from December to May
Joined now by oxlip, cowslip,
Sheltered, rarely displaced
By honesty taller then ever,
Celebrant weed that by choice seems to range
From immaculate white through magenta to purple.
Hellebore proves a Christmas-to-Whitsun rose,
The petals holding while their colours fade.
Lushly lingering, as if on a riverbank,
To verges cleared, overshadowed
Forget-me-not admixes
Reminders of watery blue, the sky's.
Late, the plum blossom ripped in its time
Bunches against the gusts
That now may carry its pollen
If the fruitflies and bees, detained,
Fail to put in their appearance,
Cherry, pear, greengage whites
Concur with the pinks of peach and apple.

Left to their ways, the wild garden's half-nature,
Deepened in early and evening light,
Almost the various, mutable hues cohere.

3

This May-Day, meanwhile, on metropolitan streets
Crowded and blocked by planned exasperation
At off-shore subsidiaries everywhere
Of the United Corporation,
Anarchy at its wit's end clinches with law-and-order –
Itself grown brashly rank, aggressive as ground elder –
Makes an event, a riotous consummation
Fit for the media synthesis of sensation,
Sterilized by the next day's horrors and despair.

4

Back, then, to humble non-events, anachronistic
Until, unless it's a deity science can clone.

After collision still, near-seasonal weather returns,
Hints at a truce between sunrays and haze.

A belated black lamb, uncloned,
By a ewe, uncloned, is suckled.
A weaned black lamb plucks at new grass.

With the less owned, less usable beings
All, for a while, may be well.

Clear sky, blue sea again, the breezes mild,
Shy deer, shy leverets grazing
As though the lost simplicities were safe in hiding,
Somewhere song-thrush, missel-thrush, lark
For deaf ears only ran through their scales,
Dubious time dissolved in the doubt.

Distinctly a cuckoo calls.
Wood pigeon, collared dove
Keep low their continuo's colloquial phrases
Marking no month, unknowably repeated.

JUNE

I

Summer's come in, all of four cloudless days,
Trees duped into their leafage, weed to thrive.
Dazzled, the mind goes blank, so does the verse:
Effulgence blinds and fulness needs no telling.
In their good garden Adam and Eve were dumb,
Being at one with what the weather was
Until it turned against them, separating,
The multiplicity lost cried out for names,

Attrition, drudgery kept a cab-horse fit
For plodding and for waiting, its condition.
Then by its owner, who'd received the news
Of their redundancy, the horse was taken
Out of its Hackney mews
Not to the knacker's but a field so large,
So goldenly green, it could not move or graze.
Was that redemption cruel?
His bags of oats ran out, synthetic fuel
Was not yet current, the poor man meant well.

As for that lore, reversed, the serpent's back,
As a small mercy, harmless legless lizard,
Slow-worm too long unseen for recognition –
One of them sliced, mistaken for a slug
Among the compost hurriedly dug in,
Another flattened to a silver bracelet
On the same tarmac on which a grass-snake basked,
The first for twenty-five years, and designed to stir
Out of such danger, coaxed by remorseful Cain.

2

Shown or not shown, hyperbolized or hidden,
In shifts, variety kept up till winter,
Roses unfold millennial history,
Successive brevities from brier, rugosa
To the mixed progeny
Of cultivars in China, Persia, France.

This climber-creeper more bramble still than rose
Masses its polyanthus button clusters
Explosively once, by riot has its way,
Tears down the trellis, overruns the plot,
Therefore cut back, often eradicated
Even from hedgerows which dog-rose, bramble, hop
Less fragrantly, less flagrantly may invade.

Slower, more selfed, those farthest from their nature,
Those open and enlarged, those packed with petals
Around a core no pollinator reaches.
Both long ago forced from primal white and pink
To a near-spectrum's shades and multicolours,
Red, purple deepened to its limit, black,
Gorse-yellow, glaring, half and quarter-yellows
Now on rice-paper, now on silk or velvet . . .

3

But leave them nameless here, to co-exist.
Bleak cloud already glowers towards Eden.
Forgoing other freedoms, retain the best,
The licence to desist.
Leave to rosarian, to rosalogist
The listing, classifying catalogue
Of the too many things that clutter, clog,
North-western wind to blow, small rain to fall
On struggling flower, conscripted animal.
The light returned will cease.

Two pairs of martins havereprieved their nests
Long crumbling under eaves,
No warbler yet has ruffled the new leaves.
With that the chronicle rests.

Hold in suspense
The discord that to us is innocence,
Tadpole all rubber gob and gut
Which on a carp's pierced side will glut,
Heron tall tomb of living fish and frog,
This radiance too in which the flux relents,
Stillness that drowns events and non-events –
Merge them in recollection of a peace.

JULY

I

A wane it is that rules this flowering,
High summer's, a descent,
Long light, brief petals with no power to cling,
Slowly evolved, prepared, but not to keep,
Even the packed, impenetrably deep
Of Gallica, Bourbon, Damask, Moss, Provence.

Look now, look hourly, so lavishly they're spent
Though never drenched or ruffled by one breeze;
Flimsier the cistus flowers – epiphanies
More instantaneous still:
Their mottled pattern splits, illegible.
Familiar foxglove, then, campanula,
The learnt by heart, plain brier – do they stay?
Hardly by repetition of the day
Gardeners labour, wait for, wearying:
Fulfilment sinks into sleep.

2

For my dead friend, searcher of silences
Through words that were not speech or song
Will it be wrong
To break a silence with words that would cohere?
Only by naming him I should intrude
As when, a stranger to him, my older friend
Who out of loneliness
Must flick quick darts that, probing, pricked, provoked,
Bantered 'Your trouble is, you've never suffered.'
And he, the reticent, austere, serene,
In rage rose from the table, tilting it,
The tea things toppled at a summer suit;
Then, hurt Achilles in his tent, sat brooding
Until sufficient silence hatched forgiveness.

Silence it was that in his words I read,
Rarely of selfhood suffered.
Small-talk at tables we have left as litter
In Texas, Mexico, 'my' Suffolk and 'his' Drôme.
Walking there, left met silences to roam,
Listening, looking for the never said.
His logic was elision, to let silence in,
A syntax of hiatus, false reason shredded.
This much I could know of him – and what we saw
    together,
Each then to work on in his own prevailing weather
Like the white-golden rose
Searched for in vain till for both gardens found:
Another silence shared on separate ground.

On what was 'his' in greater silence now it grows,
And, here, another too,
Come true from seed of one of his, mauve-red –
An archetype revealed, perfect regression? –
Denies he can be dead
While the same silence rounds that flowerhead.

3

These chronicles! Each the last
And none an ending.
Their non-events have passed
And crave more tending.
Too rich July, so crowded with the gone,
I missed the going:
Blue damsel-fly weightless on
Dark water, my unknowing.

4

When the long hours creep towards dusk, and the last
    arrival
Of swallows, house martins, swifts –
All three, for once, sand martins, too, by the sea,
Warblers inland – has consummated a summer,
    subsiding,
Wild honeysuckle it is that exhales a message
To moths more sensed than seen,
Evening primrose, weed, that answers with earthy
    brightness
A bat's wings now in the leavings of so much light,
The sky still limpid, starless
As though such effulgence had glutted
The need for luminaries far off, sterile as Mars.
Only a reddish moon, matt, no surrogate yet for day,
Hangs among leafage, the surfeit's residual fruit –

5

Ominous. Moisture gathers, thunderclap, cloudburst,
Purgation of sorts, if not yet cataclysmic,
Relief to the parched, adversity to the sated.

In London's Globe Lear is out in the storm,
Ranting again, lucidly mad.
Wimbledon is washed out: proelium interruptum
From which the sloggers learn
There is a tide outside them that can turn,
Turn public lies, a few, against the liars,
Though always, always, replacements are on the way,
To the still unaccommodated poor forked animal,
The ontically duped
From stone, bronze, ice age to the junk age, ours.
Faith, love traduced, a discoloured moon's
Rising can help, and help the dupers too:
They know not what they do,
Nor do what they say, nor say what they know
Till the skies crack a little, duplicitous weather
For the washing of royal Lear strips him real.

Red light at night,
Red light next morning:
Shepherd's delight
And shepherd's warning.
Our last, merely scenic,
Died schizophrenic.

6

Over our marshes, drained pastures
One round, puffed cloud, pure white
So close and low hung still
It seemed to belong to the land, not air.
A diving warplane on exercise
Ripped through it – a non-event, routine.

Larger, darker clouds wiped out the traces,
Buffeted sunbeams, fleeing
A tattered summer – into a summer to come? –
Wind's whirl once more, and cold
For those who looked, for those who will not look,
Blurred birdcall, rare and faint,
Fall of aborted fruit
Muddled the sense of season
With contradiction, multiplicity,
Things, words, their users all in doubt now, shifted
Out of recurrence, wrenched from their meaning.

AUGUST

I

Heavily hot at the turning
Into this month of mauveness
Purest in rosebay willow-herb,
Mere tint in hogweed's white,
Lingering pink in wild geranium,
The mallows, lagging rugosa
Less urged to desist,
To rest for a while when already
Yellow-to-crimson, the hips
Are autumn's – fainter
In hemp agrimony,
Bluer in aerial verbena,
Nettle campanula, vetch,
Deepening to purple in plum.
Yet the sun's gold hidden
This day of our golden wedding.
Within one week
Mother's and father's birth,
Their marriage, their deaths,
Hers a date kept
Forty years later.

If you set your mind on it,
She never presumed to whisper,
Dying's an easy art;
Much harder to live with your dead,
Bear with their quirks, desertions;
Bear with your living also,
Love's navel-strings twisted, stretched,
An elastic made to last.

2

So it came about – and makes no sense
In fabrications of cause and effect:
A spider's web, one among millions,
Nobody's business unless a thread
Traps a notable butterfly
Or out of a notable gut
The web was spun,
A thread adheres to a prying face
That would trace the debris in it
Of a century and a bit's –
Displacements, world wars,
Revolutions, alienations,
Diminutions, making, mending –
But find no beginning, no end,
Only concurrence, marked for its mystery,
Recurrence, if observed,
Weather permitting,
The gossamer left unbroken.

3

Walled in by leafage, from ground sodden again
The buddleia's bracts, violet-mauve, are occluded.
A city plant, from railside ramparts it sprouted,
Drew heavy blossom from centennial grime,
Gloried in stunted survival that still could breed more of
    the same,
Mixing with architecture, graffiti became
Historic, condign with utility, power:
As willow herb, rubble-fed, was when whole streets had
    gone missing,
Became an event, this flower
Exotic in origin, at a loose end in London.
Like ubiquitous sycamore then, Himalayan balsam now,
Escaped from back, front, square gardens and public parks
Into the freedom of making-do,
For planners a blotch to be sanitized, for seekers a joy.

Tree-sized here, competing with trees, fulfilled,
It calls for a balcony view –
The fragrant expanse of it, the summery hue
Massed on the level of bat's flight,
Butterflies' pasture, birds that seemed in abeyance
As if on vacation too,
About their business, though, nobody else's business
This mauve month blocked with leafage;
But recalls to a London lost one buddleia'd mind.

4

Heavy the darknesses, heavy the light,
Heavier than autumn's this vacation month's,
Season of travel, escape
From ripening seed capsule, fruit,
Fulness preparing to fall.

Under grasses bending with tallness
A stoat lay dead
Of no visible wound,
The grey and white pelt
Still sleek, the limbs curled
As for sleep with open eyes –
Before bluebottles, bugs
Made a meal and nursery
Of their obduction, reduction.

Nearby our cat, senescent,
Had spent the night unharmed.
No cry of killer or killed,
No sound had roused us sleepers
Too heavy perhaps with labour done
For the ancient house refurnished,
The ancient plot replanted
So that, passed on,
They might be marked once more –
Weather permitting,
Cobwebs remaining,
Their makers gone.

5

Driven from the north-west, cloud archipelagos
Now alpine-white, now black, discharging
Rain, on the neighbouring village only
Hailstones that lay there thick,
Contracted to mornings all drab again, evenings dankly
    chill
With wood-fires perversely lit.
Withered, the mauves not of heather are quenched,
Fade from our seeing.
House martins, two pairs increased to a flock,
Perch on a wire, play musical chairs, portending
Their passage out or back to their other precarious home.

To the cat it's a summer yet, this that could be her last:
House-bound in winter, hour after hour she sits
On a bed of hay, gazing
Into leafage still rich and the dark within it,
Into her circle of years no cloudburst or thunderclap
Can break now, her home before and after,
Hardly will stir from it for food or comfort
Though she's limber enough to climb, leap and pounce;
But as if to confirm a bond, the other,
From silence kept for a lifetime
More often now will utter
Hints at least to an alien familiar host
Of the little there was to be said between them, ever.

SEPTEMBER

I

On the mauve month's last day another death,
His from infancy close, more and more distant
Since war-time dispersion, divided ways
Till scarcely one spoken or written word exchanged
Could reach a meeting-place
Where the mere tokens buzz and have no meaning;
Racked into peace now, released,
The man reluctantly public
By taking, then by giving,
In which perhaps fulfilled, a posthumous living;
Or else the truant schoolboy still lonesomely riding
Underground escalators descending, ascending
Always away, so as not to arrive
At the station that might have been his.

And X, my earliest fellow
In the seekers' and losers' trade
Gasps on the telephone,
Not ill, he says, only dying,
The unnoticed work kept up till his eighty-eighth year
Not finished, not quite, suspended.
Oh, nothing is ever ended
For us, I don't answer, old friend.

2

Late myrtle's little moonflowers, easily missed,
From pinhead buds among wild berry foliage
So starrily pale, so suddenly will open
Hazed white, galactic, hardly more than guessed,
Unearthly such a blossoming would seem
But for the redolence,
Patchouli scent left in an emptying room –
Those dark leaves evergreen, far stars more likely to last.
Seeing them, though, with eyes that slip out of time,
Surprised again by auras the scent recalls,
Giddies a chronicler whirled
From death-in-life to life-in-death, revolving.

Now *you* quit, prettily . . . a voice repeats
From out of this canopy of mortal crests,
Woodpigeon's vocables I mistranslate
And on wide muted wings
A tawny owl glides from some hidden perch.

No, I don't answer, in half-light I'll labour on

3

While the fine fibres tear,
Frail fabric of relation.
Mementoes hang on walls already bare.
Still I must plant and sow,
Clear a small space for that I cannot know
Nor own unless by shared continuation.

4

And here once more on a sun-dappled patch
Cleared of ground elder roots
One twenty-five-year-old cyclamen corm, exotic,
Kindles two hundred flowers
Against an almost overshadowing yew,
Blackness that has not killed but sheltered it.

5

Let the slow tree spread and grow,
Quick petals glint and go,
Faster, these autumn-coloured feathers
Pass with the winds of mere elusive weathers
Long become seasonless –
Predator was the hint, night bird the guess.
All's mixed now, dark with day,
First things with last, the teller struck astray

6

By events and would-be events, sheer instants – the single
    death
In which a destiny could be traced, a meaning,
And the collective grouse-shoot with killings only counted.

A rhythm breaks on our turning earth, in the spheres,
The markets crumble, power's power-house is gutted,
Administrators, panicking, scatter
To gather again for retribution
They promise will right the wrongs inexplicably perpetrated
By those they have wronged into madness,
Confirming the cause of the wrong by exacerbation,
The righting of it in promiscuous war:
Unseeing eye for unseeing eye,
Snarling tooth for snarling or smiling tooth,
Cycle more barren always
Than the maimed globe's revolving now

This winterly September, here, the skies black,
Rainstorms rushing to strip the branches still greenly leaved,
Rip off the still ripening fruit from stalks not brittle,
A squirrel, panicking, for gluttony or for store
All the slow walnut tree's borne in defiance of weathers,
Rot rosebuds belatedly forming
Where the riverlet swells with brown water,
On pastures bogged one swollen sheep lifts
A bloodied head half sliced off, and limps on,
Labouring love, too variously thwarted, aborted
Of the new flood warning makes FLOOD, THE FLOOD . . .

7

Silence . . . hiatus . . . rest . . .
Until, empty enough, in emptiness we can settle:

Light, any light remaining,
Air, any air to be breathed,
Time, any time not a respite,
Space, any space less cramping
A survivor raised from rubble
Receives as never since birth
And will lose again in contingency, even love's,
Before the completed dying
That labouring love postponed.

OCTOBER

I

Red light in the morning. But at last one day's
Unbroken radiance before the turn
Of month and leaves and more than leaves brought home
The weather waited, worked for. Some leaves have turned,
Gold in the beech-tops, others have fallen,
Late or obstinate flowers responded to any light –
Colchicum pink, then white, less pale, nerine.
Evening primrose steadfastly has linked
Dusk half-light to the dawn's, shining through mist.
Contrary kinship rounds
Even this year, connects
Cowering aconite's earliest yellow
With tall monkshood's concluding blue.

2

Gale warning, that red light? Prayers here and there
That if a little wild, unmannerly,
No terrorist, this one will not exceed
The speed limit set of seventy miles per hour.
Hurricane veterans, housed in half-ruins,
Though wearying, hone their rusted metal,
Ready again for maintenance, the price to be paid,
A potential bonus too:
Wind-aided clearance of the laden orchard
In the apple-picking now to be done,
Fewer to store for keeping,
The more made over
To residual friends, to strangers,
To squirrel, fieldmouse, blackbird, earwig, soil.
Loss, waste to whom? None to a curious grower
Of thirty-five unmarketable kinds:
Once seen and savoured, what they were they are
And the sound stock will hold.

3

Clearance, management, ever since Adam and Eve
Repetitive, arduous, nasty, necessary
Of more than enough, of all that overhangs,
Crowds out or, overshadowing, sickens
The rare, the delicate, the merely slow.
One summer's foliage starved of full light,
Heart-wood, root may perish.
Since Cain and Abel never has agri-, horti-,
What-have-you-culture rid itself of the meddling
This month demands. Ambivalence has reigned.
Not choosing to choose, among mysteries, we must,
Choosing the worst are marked, elected, blessed.
Endless this lopping, sawing, scything, felling seems
Which, though for letting-be, grim art imposes,
For love, for goodness, freedom's sake, for nature.
Else you and I step out one morning
And 'Where's the garden?' cry,
'Marsh, field, hedged farm horizon on which the eye
For its own scope and limits could rely?'

So lugging, wheel-barrowing of lumber bare,
Cankered or rank, cut back – unlike our trash
Reducible to compost or clean ash
That once again will feed
The same mutated and recycled need,
With wood-smoke, weed-smoke spices the emptying air.

4

Waning, the days grow warmer,
Mornings are white with mist
Long after muffled cock-crow
In stillness so heavy
That a rook's flight seems outmoded,
As though air so thick would never again be fit
For the passage of animate bodies not cased in plastic,
As though whatever flies
Were power packed in lies –

Passenger 'planes converted into missiles,
Missiles, bombs mixed
With ideological food drops
On to rubble, rock, the survivors
Of ideological war, so continuous
That one became like another:
Mixed motives, mixed means, mixed ends
Deadlocked in drought, starvation.

An old shepherd, listening, laughs:
Come down, dear avengers,
And you could learn how to die.
Won't your expensive egos
Condescend to slow weavers of rugs?
But the poisons are homing now:
Your tormentor is one of your kind.
And our desperate contribution
To your global order
Is opium poppies raised
For your kind's profit, less than our subsistence
While our food runs out.
We also are learning, you'll see:

*Unreal trades, unreal skills,
Mobility bland, blind and deaf,
Mobile money's twitchings,
Its incestuous procreation,
Manic fear that overkills.*

*Or fly higher, beyond
Your suspects' hiding-place,
Transcend them, leave behind
Us and this earth you have botched.
A would-be sage among you
Has advised you: Emigrate
To another planet, and soon.
If evolved for outer space,
More fit for the sterile stars,
Go there, take off, post-human,
For synthetic-air-conditioned
Supercities on Mars,
Big deals on the cold moon.*

5

By mid-morning a dim disc,
Spectral sun, glimmers
Through moisture resistant, persistent.
A leaf trembles, a butterfly
On tremulous wings
Emerges, dares to rise.

NOVEMBER

I

At the turn of one more month,
Full moon, air-stream about to veer,
Another single day
Of might-have-been summer.

Might-have-been is for children,
These, too, being ripped from their mothers,
Not here, by those who declared
War without end, amen, meaning
They're the marshals of might-have-been,
Never-was, never-will-be,
Of dithering carnage multiplied
While they haggle, squabble, gabble
Over the spoils,
Spoils of the spoiled earth,
Oil from her entrails, cruel fuel,
Murderous therm.
At gobbets disdained, the scraps,
Words, carrion flies
Buzz to breed there, to spread.
That's for a start. Trust your leaders:
We've seen next to nothing yet.

Harsher winds, though, can cleanse:
On to leaves whirling,
Bare branches exposed
The riven sky shines.

2

Towards winter land cares dwindle,
Dissolve in the lessening days.
Skies widen, sea colours respond
When the cloud-mass, breaking
Hints at islanded blue
Such as to Arctic, Antarctic, high mountain ice
Lured questing intruders
Merged in that ice-light's blueness.

This apple-tree, centenarian,
Hollowing, bore both fruit
And mistletoe yearly cut,
Till fungus dug deeper.
Without commemoration
Promptly it was dismembered,
Felled and logged for the grate:
Light, more light, where it fell,
Light again from the burning –
More than warmth to those with the frost inside them –
One essence exhaled into air.

Perfumed finery left on the lane's verge,
This belated meadowsweet's frothy head
Seems to mope in remembrance
Until one ray jolts it back
Into merely being,
No matter that it has lasted
While the whole marsh withered,
Fallen sweet chestnuts rot into sodden grass.

3

Among the litter now
Lie rose petals never noticed
When, out of season, they clung
To climbers high up on the house
Or the cherry-tree turning, half-stripped.
Small maples make a show,
A sundown of their going,
Too late, too early viburnum's
Blossoming makes a birth;
But from dawn to dusk,
Horizon to zenith
Clouded or clear
All by sheer light are outshone.

4

And these non-events – your last? –
To what end do they tend?
To none, by their nature, none
As long as one surface can shine.

The doers change and the done,
But to light, only light, I leave
The next weather, next word:
Light, however cold
From a source not yours, not mine,
Reflected, deflected, deferred,
Withheld, occluded, untold:
Spark innate in a blind eye,
Glint of anima, animal's eye,
Flicker of flame in a cave,
Glitter of crystal in rock,
Phosphorescence in water,
Palest of sunbeams, moonbeams,
Dubious gleam of a star –
Still for a passing surpassed.

5

White, silvery light
Takes back the tatters,
Fluttering leaves held upturned
On the white poplar's crest
So bright that their unmaking
Flowers as never their spring.

Darkened now beyond crimson
To the brink of blackness
Where no dapple hankers for day,
The silver maple's, detained,
In effulgence meet their night,
The white light receives all their shades.

Some new and recent poetry from Anvil

GAVIN BANTOCK
Just Think of It

OLIVER BERNARD
Verse &c.

NINA BOGIN
The Winter Orchards

PETER DALE
Under the Breath

DICK DAVIS
Belonging

HARRY GUEST
A Puzzling Harvest
COLLECTED POEMS 1955–2000

JAMES HARPUR
Oracle Bones

PHILIP HOLMES
Lighting the Steps

E A MARKHAM
A Rough Climate

DENNIS O'DRISCOLL
Exemplary Damages

SALLY PURCELL
Collected Poems

GRETA STODDART
At Home in the Dark

JULIAN TURNER
Crossing the Outskirts

DANIEL WEISSBORT
Letters to Ted

Some poetry in translation from Anvil

JOSEP CARNER: *Nabí*
Translated by J L Gili

GOETHE: *Roman Elegies and other poems*
Translated by Michael Hamburger

NIKOLAY GUMILYOV: *The Pillar of Fire*
Translated by Richard McKane

YEHUDA HALEVI: *Poems from the Diwan*
Translated by Gabriel Levin

NÂZIM HİKMET: *Beyond the Walls*
Translated by Ruth Christie and Richard McKane

PETER HUCHEL: *The Garden of Theophrastus*
Translated by Michael Hamburger

VICTOR HUGO: *The Distance, The Shadows*
Translated by Harry Guest

POEMS OF JULES LAFORGUE
POEMS OF FRANÇOIS VILLON
Translated by Peter Dale

FEDERICO GARCÍA LORCA: *A Season in Granada*
Edited and translated by Christopher Maurer

FRIEDRICH NIETZSCHE: *Dithyrambs of Dionysus*
Translated by R J Hollingdale

PO CHÜ-I: *The Selected Poems of Po Chü-i*
Translated by David Hinton

RAINER MARIA RILKE: *Turning-Point*
Translated by Michael Hamburger

RABINDRANATH TAGORE: *Song Offerings*
(Gitanjali)
Translated by Joe Winter